The Accounting Cycle

A Primer for Nonfinancial Managers

Revised Edition

Jay L. Jacquet and William C. Miller, Jr.

A Fifty-Minute™ Series Book

The Accounting Cycle

A Primer for Nonfinancial Managers

Revised Edition

Jay L. Jacquet and
William C. Miller, Jr.

CREDITS:
Senior Editor: **Debbie Woodbury**
Assistant Editor: **Genevieve Del Rosario**
Production Manager: **Denise Powers**
Design: **Nicole Phillips**
Production Artist: **Zach Hooker**
Cartoonist: **Ralph Mapson**

For more information contact:

Course Technology
25 Thomson Place
Boston, MA 02210

Or find us on the Web at **www.courseilt.com**

For permission to use material from this text or product, submit a request online at www.thomsonrights.com.

ISBN 1-56052-667-X
Library of Congress Catalog Card Number 20011099373
Printed in Canada by Webcom Limited

5 6 7 8 9 PM 06 05 04

Learning Objectives For:

THE ACCOUNTING CYCLE

The objectives for *The Accounting Cycle, Revised Edition* are listed below. They have been developed to guide you, the reader, to the core issues covered in this book.

THE OBJECTIVES OF THIS BOOK ARE:

❑ 1) To discuss recordkeeping systems

❑ 2) To review the vocabulary of accounting

❑ 3) To explain making adjusting and closing entries

❑ 4) To discuss accounting decision making

ASSESSING YOUR PROGRESS

In addition to the learning objectives above, Course Technology has developed a Crisp Series **assessment** that covers the fundamental information presented in this book. A 25-item, multiple-choice and true/false questionnaire allows the reader to evaluate his or her comprehension of the subject matter. To buy the assessment and answer key, go to www.courseilt.com and search on the book title or via the assessment format, or call 1-800-442-7477.

Assessments should not be used in any employee selection process.

About the Authors

Jay L. Jacquet is Associate Professor in business at Central Ohio Technical College in Newark, Ohio. He holds a B.B.A., BusEd, and M.B.A. from the University of Toledo. Jay has been Chair of the business division at Central Ohio Technical College and has taught at a number of colleges. He continues to consult and holds a public accounting license in Ohio.

William C. Miller, Jr. is Vice President of Business Services at North Central State College in Mansfield, Ohio. He holds a B.S. degree and M.B.A. from Ashland University. Bill has been Dean of the College of Business at North Central State and has taught at a number of colleges. He continues to consult and practice public accounting services.

How to Use This Book

This *Fifty-Minute™ Series Book* is a unique, user-friendly product. As you read through the material, you will quickly experience the interactive nature of the book. There are numerous exercises, real-world case studies, and examples that invite your opinion, as well as checklists, tips, and concise summaries that reinforce your understanding of the concepts presented.

A Crisp Learning *Fifty-Minute™ Book* can be used in a variety of ways. Individual self-study is one of the most common. However, many organizations use *Fifty-Minute* books for pre-study before a classroom training session. Other organizations use the books as a part of a systemwide learning program—supported by video and other media based on the content in the books. Still others work with Crisp Learning to customize the material to meet their specific needs and reflect their culture. Regardless of how it is used, we hope you will join the more than 20 million satisfied learners worldwide who have completed a *Fifty-Minute Book*.

Preface

Every business needs a basic recordkeeping system. This book was written to explain the fundamentals of accounting to those who have had little or no accounting experience or training. It begins by explaining the basics of business transactions and finishes with closing entries.

The Accounting Cycle is not complicated. Much of the vocabulary of accounting has made the system hard to understand. In this text, we have made every effort to clear up basic learning hurdles. We have written it as a stand-alone aid on accounting basics or as a supplement to a standard, beginning accounting text. This is not a comprehensive fundamentals of accounting book. However, all the concepts represented here can generally be applied to every business transaction.

We urge you to follow the examples and complete the self-tests. Reviews are provided at the end of each section. Practice and use of the basic concepts is the foundation of learning these techniques. When you complete this book you should have a basic understanding of accounting and be able to use this knowledge to understand the financial position of your business.

Please take your time and have fun!

Jay L. Jacquet

William C. Miller, Jr.

Contents

Part 6: Closing Entries

Part 7: The Balance Sheet and Income Statement

Part 8: Special Consideration: Inventory

Part 9: Business Decisions

Appendix

Introduction

Accounting: What Is It?

Bookkeeping is the practice of recording the transactions of a business. Accounting is the bookkeeping methodology involved in creating a financial record of business transactions and in preparing statements concerning the assets, liabilities, and operating results of a business. Accounting requires the recording and summarizing of business and financial transactions. The information then needs to be analyzed and verified and the results reported through financial statements.

Accounting is a two-step process:

Step 1: Choose the right accounts used in a transaction.

Step 2: Determine the correct amount to be used in the transactions.

Both of these steps are critical to successful recordkeeping.

As you go through this book, you may notice that we have not included dollar amounts. We want you to answer the basic question "Where do I put it?" before getting burdened down with trying to calculate the amounts. It does not matter whether or not you determine the correct amount, if you place it in the wrong account. Once you are familiar with the recordkeeping system, dollar amounts can be added. In the beginning, the vocabulary of accounting and different accounts will be enough to understand.

Some Accounting Concepts and Principles

A few "rules of the road" should be followed in preparing financial data. These concepts and principles apply for all businesses.

Business-entity concept

Checkbook		Checkbook
Personal		**Business**

A business should be a separate entity from the owners of the business. Personal items or assets should not be listed as business assets. Records and transactions of the business are separate.

Continuing-concern concept	The business will continue to operate. This concept allows all business assets (property) to be recorded at cost and remain at that figure no matter what the market value may be. If the company were to be sold, the assets of the company would be valued at market to determine the selling price of the business.
Time-period concept	This divides the business into equal periods of time, such as a month, a quarter, or a year.
Cost principle	Assets are carried on the financial statements of the company at cost. In most cases, cost is what is paid for the asset. However, if the file cabinet used at your home was then brought into the business, it would be recorded at what the business would have paid for a used file cabinet.
Matching principle	If earnings and expenses are to be compared in an accounting period, they need to be recorded when one benefits the other. The income from September is matched with the expenses for September.
Consistency principle	Methods and procedures need to be kept the same over time. This principle allows for better comparison of data collected in business. If methods and procedures are changed, the business must show this change, and the effect of this change, on the financial statements.

x

Overview of the Accounting Cycle

2

The Accounting Cycle

The entire accounting cycle of a business is shown below. Business transactions are recorded in a *journal*, during the month. At the end of the month, *adjusting entries* are prepared and placed in the journal. A final set of *closing entries* are then placed in the *journal*, and the *financial statements* are prepared. The process begins again for the next accounting period.

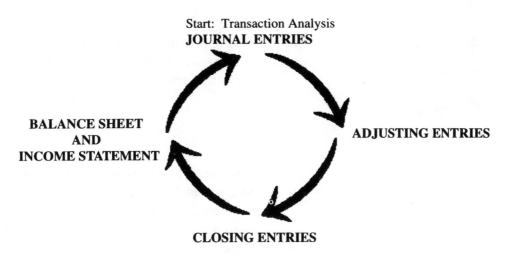

Start: Transaction Analysis
JOURNAL ENTRIES

ADJUSTING ENTRIES

CLOSING ENTRIES

BALANCE SHEET AND INCOME STATEMENT

Adjusting Entries   These are entries to assign revenue and expenses in the period incurred. These additional month-end entries match expired costs and unrecorded revenues to the period.

Balance Sheet   A "snapshot" of the business' assets, liabilities, and owner's equity (also known as "net worth"). Assets are property. Liabilities are what is owed. Owner's equity is the difference between the assets and liabilities.

Income Statement   The profit or loss of a business, based on earnings less expenses. This statement reflects a period of time (usually one month).

Closing Entries   Entries made to zero balance all temporary accounts at the end of the accounting period. (Temporary accounts are discussed on page 8.)

Journal   The book of original entry. All transactions are recorded here first.

Transactions   Business papers and source documents.

Steps in the Accounting Cycle

Step 1. Business transactions are created.
Source documents are created: receipts, bills and checks.

Book of Original Entry:
Transactions are recorded here first.

Journal

Step 2. Analyze and record the transaction.
Information is placed in the journal by account name.

Post

Ledger

Cash

Accounts Payable

Step 3. Post (copy) the information from the journal to the ledger.
Information from the journal is recorded into the general ledger (book in which accounts are recorded).

Transactions that occur frequently are grouped together into accounts such as cash, equipment, and accounts payable.

Step 4. Prepare a trial balance.
The trial balance is a listing of balances in the accounts of the general ledger in order of assets, liabilities, owner's equity, revenue, and expense accounts.

Trial Balance

Assets
Liabilities
Owner's Equity
Revenue
Expenses

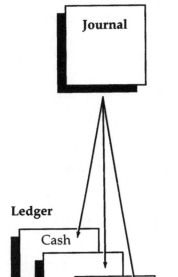

Journal

Ledger

Cash

Accounts
Payable

Step 5. Journalize adjusting entries.
There are no source documents. Adjusting entries are completed at the end of the accounting period to match the proper revenue with expense in that period.

Step 6. Post (copy) adjustments from the journal to the ledger.
Adjusting entries from the journal are recorded into the general ledger.

Step 7. Prepare an adjusted trial balance.
The adjusted trial balance reflects only adjusting entries. If an error has occurred, we know it was made in the posting of adjusting entries, because the trial balance was prepared at the end of the month.

**Adjusted
Trial
Balance**

STEPS IN THE ACCOUNTING CYCLE (CONTINUED)

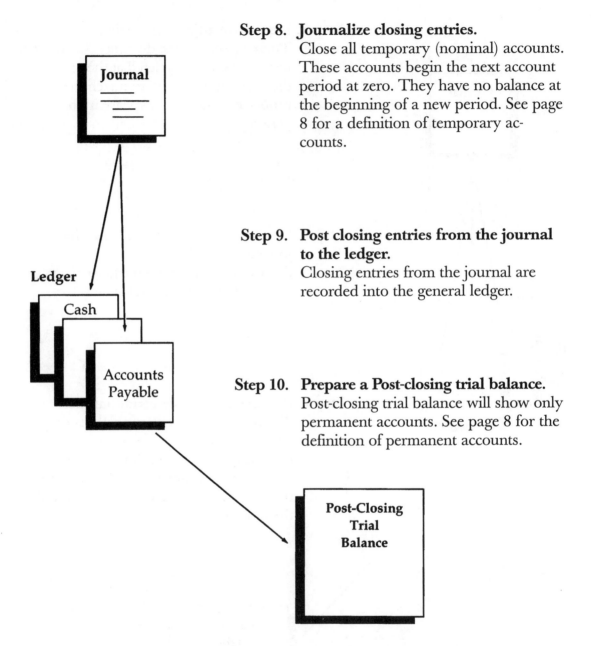

Step 8. Journalize closing entries.
Close all temporary (nominal) accounts. These accounts begin the next account period at zero. They have no balance at the beginning of a new period. See page 8 for a definition of temporary accounts.

Step 9. Post closing entries from the journal to the ledger.
Closing entries from the journal are recorded into the general ledger.

Step 10. Prepare a Post-closing trial balance.
Post-closing trial balance will show only permanent accounts. See page 8 for the definition of permanent accounts.

Step 11. Prepare the Financial Statements
The two basic statements are the Income Statement and Balance Sheet.

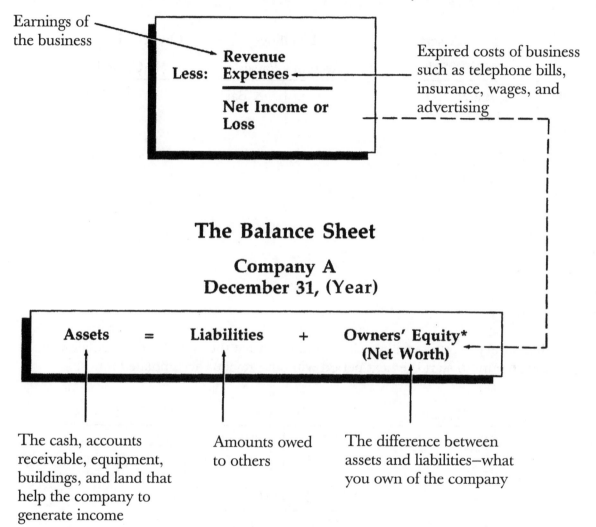

The Income Statement

For the Month Ended December 31, (Year)

Earnings of
the business

Revenue

Less: Expenses

Net Income or
Loss

Expired costs of business
such as telephone bills,
insurance, wages, and
advertising

The Balance Sheet

Company A
December 31, (Year)

Assets   =   Liabilities   +   Owners' Equity*
(Net Worth)

The cash, accounts
receivable, equipment,
buildings, and land that
help the company to
generate income

Amounts owed
to others

The difference between
assets and liabilities—what
you own of the company

**The Balance Sheet equation cannot balance until net income or loss is added to the Balance Sheet from the
Income Statement. The movement of this profit or loss is completed through closing entries (see Part 6).*

Temporary and Permanent Accounts

Permanent accounts are accounts that are not closed at the end of the period. These are Balance Sheet accounts (except for withdrawals). They carry current balances as long as the business continues.

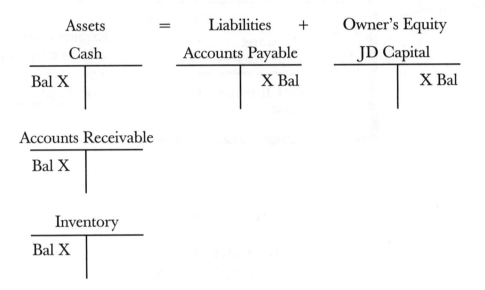

Temporary accounts will be closed out to zero at the end of the period allowing the account to start the next period without previous accumulated funds.

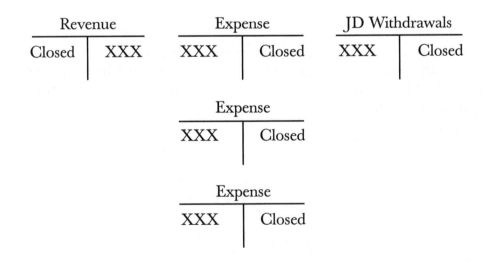

The Income Statement
For the Month Ended December 31, (Year)

Revenue
Less: Expenses

Net Income or
Loss

Revenue, expenses, and withdrawals are called temporary (nominal) accounts. These accounts are closed at the end of an accounting period.

The Balance Sheet
Company A
December 31, (Year)

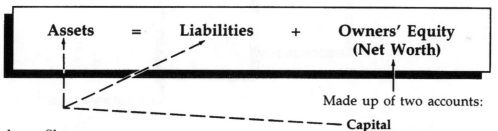

Assets = **Liabilities** + **Owners' Equity (Net Worth)**

Made up of two accounts:
Capital
Withdrawals

Balance Sheet accounts (except for withdrawals) are called permanent (real) accounts. They carry current balances, as long as the business continues.

The capital account is used to place money in the business that belongs to you personally.

The withdrawal account is used to take the owner's salary and other assets from the business for personal use.

Review

Monthly Transactions

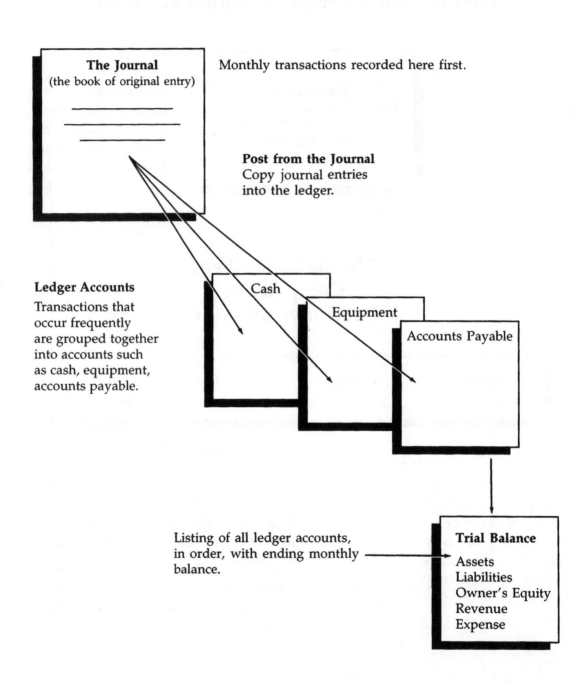

The Journal
(the book of original entry)

Monthly transactions recorded here first.

Post from the Journal
Copy journal entries
into the ledger.

Ledger Accounts

Transactions that
occur frequently
are grouped together
into accounts such
as cash, equipment,
accounts payable.

Cash

Equipment

Accounts Payable

Listing of all ledger accounts,
in order, with ending monthly
balance.

Trial Balance

Assets
Liabilities
Owner's Equity
Revenue
Expense

Adjusting Entries

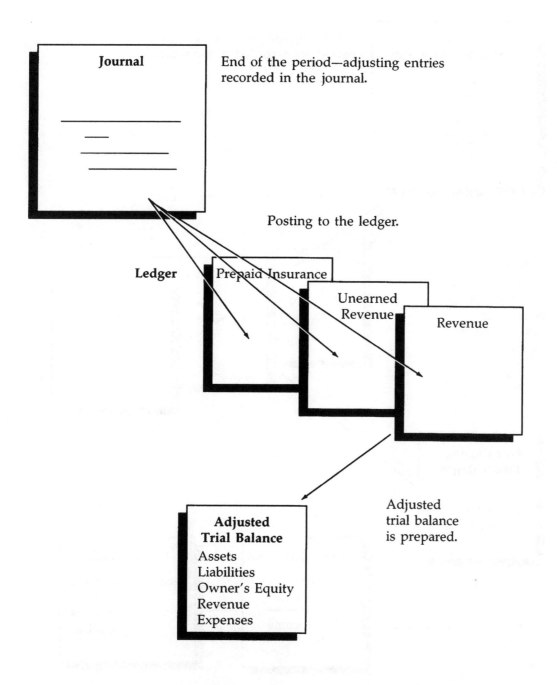

Journal

End of the period—adjusting entries recorded in the journal.

Posting to the ledger.

Ledger Prepaid Insurance

Unearned Revenue

Revenue

Adjusted Trial Balance
Assets
Liabilities
Owner's Equity
Revenue
Expenses

Adjusted trial balance is prepared.

Closing Entries

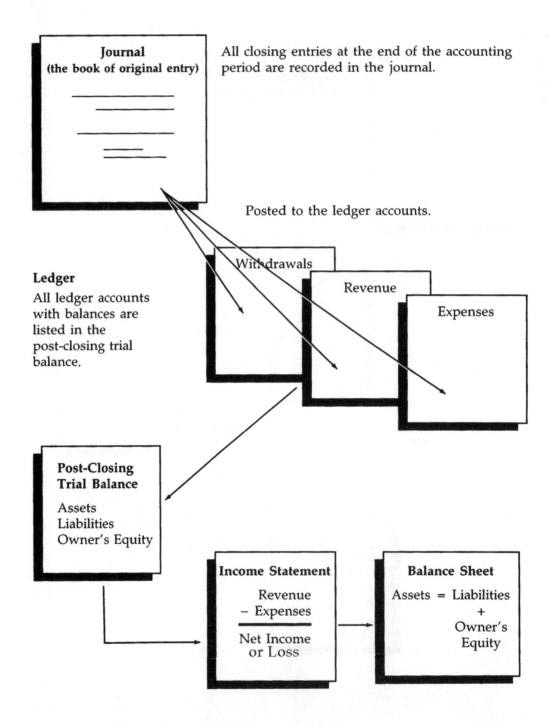

Journal
(the book of original entry)

All closing entries at the end of the accounting period are recorded in the journal.

Posted to the ledger accounts.

Withdrawals

Revenue

Expenses

Ledger
All ledger accounts with balances are listed in the post-closing trial balance.

Post-Closing Trial Balance

Assets
Liabilities
Owner's Equity

Income Statement

Revenue
– Expenses
_____
Net Income
or Loss

Balance Sheet

Assets = Liabilities
+
Owner's
Equity

Cash or Accrual

Accounting?

14

Cash or Accrual Accounting?

A business can record revenue (earnings) and expenses in one of two ways. The cash and accrual bases of recordkeeping define revenue and expenses in different ways.

The *cash* basis of accounting records revenue and expense as the business owner pays for them. The net income (difference between revenue and expenses) of the company is determined by subtracting *cash out* from *cash in*.

The *accrual* basis of accounting attempts to place earnings and expenses in the same month, based on the *matching principle*. Cash is not necessarily the same as revenue. Under the accrual system, revenue is recorded when earned.

Notice on the tax form (Schedule C) below, the first question asked of the sole proprietor (single owner) is which accounting method the company will use. The methods are cash, accrual, or other. The "other" method can be a combination of the two systems. The cash method can be used for expenses and revenue. The accrual can be used for inventory.

SCHEDULE C (Form 1040)	**Profit or Loss From Business** (Sole Proprietorship)	OMB No. 1545-0074
Department of the Treasury Internal Revenue Service (99)	▶ Partnerships, joint ventures, etc., must file Form 1065 or Form 1065-B. ▶ Attach to Form 1040 or Form 1041. ▶ See instructions for Schedule C (Form 1040).	**2000** Attachment Sequence No. 09

Name of proprietor	Social security number (SSN)

A Principal business or profession, including product or service (see instructions)	B Enter code from Instructions ▶
C Business name. If no separate business name, leave blank.	D Employer ID number (EIN), If any

E Business address (including suite or room no.) ▶ _____
City, town or post office, state, and ZIP code

F Accounting method: (1) [X] Cash (2) [ ] Accrual (3) [ ] Other (specify) ▶ _____

16

The Cash Basis of Recording Earnings

A majority of small businesses use the cash method of accounting. It is simple to understand. Record the earnings of the business only when the cash is received. All expenses are recorded when the check or cash is issued. Payments are considered made when they are mailed. Under the cash method, credit card charges are considered paid when you sign for them, not when you pay the bill. You may use a combination of the cash method and accrual method if this combination clearly shows your income and expense transactions and is used consistently. A business owner cannot switch between cash, accrual, or combination accounting.

The Accrual Basis of Recording Earnings

Accrual accounting is a more difficult system to understand because it involves the timing of revenue and expenses. This timing may have nothing to do with the payments or receiving of cash. Revenue is recorded when it has been earned, and expenses are recorded when they are incurred, whether they are paid or not paid. Accrual basis accounting should be used in all cases in which the production, purchase, and sale of merchandise is a factor in revenue. This would include inventories, described in Part 8. The major differences between the cash and accrual methods of recording revenue and expenses are illustrated in the following example:

Jennifer owns a consulting company. In January she earned $4,000, but received only $1,500 in cash. At the same time, her expenses were:

Rent: $1,500, which she paid
Advertising: $500, which she did not pay
Utilities: $250, which she paid
Miscellaneous: $50, which she paid
Office supplies: $100, which she did not pay

All earnings / Only cash

	Accrual Accounting	Cash Accounting
Revenue	$4,000	$1,500
Expenses:		
Rent	1,500	1,500
Advertising	500	0
Utilities	250	250
Miscellaneous	50	50
Office supplies	100	0
Net Income	$1,600	Net Loss ($300)

Not Paid

Note: There is a $1,900 difference between methods

SELF-TEST 1: CASH VS. ACCRUAL ACCOUNTING

Record the following revenue and expenses in the appropriate column.

The Consulting Company

In June the company earned $8,000, but received only $3,500 in cash. At the same time, expenses were:

Rent: $1,000, was paid
Wage expense: $1,200, of which only 1/2 was paid
Utilities expense: $300 was paid
Equipment expense: $500 was unpaid
Miscellaneous expense: $100 was paid
Office supplies: $200 was unpaid

	Accrual Accounting	Cash Accounting
Revenue		
Expenses:		
Rent		
Wage		
Utilities		
Equipment		
Miscellaneous		
Office Supplies		
Net Profit or (Loss)		

If you have any problems with the solutions to this self-test, please review the previous sections.

Check your answers with the author's solutions in the Appendix.

Review

Remember, the difference between the accrual and cash methods is in the *recognition* of earnings and expenses.

Accrual Method   Revenue and expenses are recognized when earned or incurred.

Cash Method   Revenue is recorded on the books only when cash is received and expenses are recorded when cash is spent.

You may use a combination of the cash and accrual methods. In Part 8 of this book, we talk about businesses with inventory. In this case, you would be required to keep inventory on the accrual basis, even though all other income and expense items could be kept on the cash method.

Basic

Recordkeeping

Systems

Setting Up the Books

All accounting transactions need to be recorded in a systematic recordkeeping system. This recordkeeping system has five basic categories (indicated below by the circled numbers) in which these transactions are recorded. The five categories come from the two financial reports, the income statement and the balance sheet, which we prepare at the end of accounting periods.

**The Balance Sheet
Company A
December 31, (Year)**

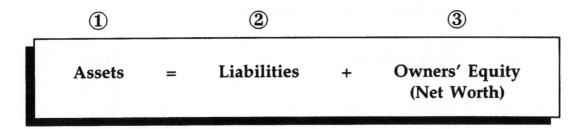

①	②	③
Assets =	Liabilities +	Owners' Equity (Net Worth)

**The Income Statement
For the Month Ended December 31, (Year)**

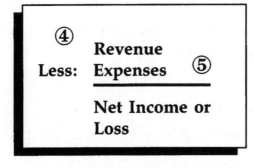

④
Revenue
Less: Expenses ⑤

Net Income or Loss

The Chart of Accounts

After we have determined which of the five categories are affected by a business transaction, we need to determine to what account the transaction should apply. These accounts will change with each company's needs. At some point, the business may need to add more accounts. The number of accounts will be determined by grouping similar transactions together.

Chart of Accounts

Assets	= Liabilities	+ Owner's Equity	Revenue	Expenses
Cash	Accounts Payable	Capital	Earnings	Wage
Accounts/ Receivable	Note Payable	Withdrawals		Utilities
Automobile	Mortgage Payable			Supplies
Equipment				Repair
Building				Rent
Land				Office
				Interest
				Insurance
				Advertising

Steps in Recording Business Transactions

Step 1: Know the five basic categories: assets, liabilities, owner's equity, revenue, and expense accounts.

Step 2: Develop a chart of accounts for your business.

Step 3: Record business transactions:

> ➤ Recognize key words in a business transaction

> ➤ Choose categories for each transaction

> ➤ Choose the accounts under the categories

Key Word Recognition

No matter what accounting system your business uses, double- or single-entry, you must be able to recognize the key words in a business transaction. Here are some examples:

1. **Invested cash** in the business firm.
   (Placed your money in the firm. This is not money the business earned.)

2. Purchased **office equipment on account.**
   (Bought office equipment on credit. This is a liability of your company.)

3. **Paid** for **personal telephone calls** with a business check.
   (Paid for nonbusiness calls on your business phone. This will not be a business expense of the firm.)

4. Purchased **office supplies** and **office equipment on account.**
   (Bought office supplies and office equipment on credit.)

5. Purchased **office supplies** with **cash.**
   (Paid cash for office supplies.)

6. **Paid** the **rent** for the month.
   (Paid cash for the rental of the building space.)

7. **Invested** your used **truck** in the business.
   (Placed a truck in the business, which was your personal truck.)

8. Performed **accounting services on account.**
   (Performed accounting work and did not receive payment.)

9. **Paid off** part of the supplies and office equipment in #4.
   (Paid part of the bill, reducing the liability of the company.)

10. **Paid** the **business' telephone bill.**
    (A check was written for the business telephone bill.)

SELF-TEST 2: KEY WORD RECOGNITION

Analyze the following transactions and underline the key words.

Example:

Invested <u>cash</u>, <u>an</u> <u>automobile</u> and <u>office</u> <u>equipment</u> in the business.

1. Performed services for a client for cash.

2. Performed services for a client on account.

3. Paid the secretaries' wages.

4. Paid the utilities bill.

5. Collected the cash on the account in transaction #2.

6. Paid a three-year insurance policy.

7. Invested cash in the business.

8. Performed services on account.

9. Paid the telephone bill.

10. Purchased office equipment for cash and the remainder on account.

If you have any problems with the solutions to this self-test, please review the previous sections.

Check your answers with the author's solutions in the Appendix.

Single-Entry Recordkeeping

Single-entry recordkeeping has been used for a long time. It is easy to use. A good rule of thumb in using a single-entry system is the number of checks written per month. If you write 30 checks or less per month, consider using the single-entry system.

Many single-entry accounting systems are on the market for the small businessperson. They are primarily used in cash basis accounting. These systems can be purchased from business-form distributors and business mail order form companies.

The single-entry system allows the business owner to write a check and record the amount in a journal at the same time. This is done by placing a carbon strip on the back of the check. As the check is written, the information is reproduced in the journal.

A Single-Entry System, Using the Business Checkbook

Your personal checkbook is an excellent example of a single-entry recordkeeping system. The concept of single entry can also apply to the use of the business owner's checkbook. After you have written the check and amount on the first line, you identify the account to which that check would apply. Remember, under a single-entry cash system, the recording of an entry occurs when cash comes in or goes out.

CHECK REGISTER

Number	Date 199X	Description of the Transaction	Payment		✓	Deposit		Balance	
								$4,000	00
106	1/12	WILLIAM MILLER	600	00				3,400	00
		RENT EXPENSE							
	1/16	DEPOSIT				100	00	3,500	00
		REVENUE							

Example of a single-entry system. Rent expense is the account charged for $600.

In this example, $100 was earned by the business and deposited for the day.

Double-Entry Accounting

The double-entry system requires the use of two or more accounts for each business transaction. As your business begins to grow, some transactions will include more than cash in or cash out. Your company will outgrow the single-entry system.

Example: *Invested office equipment and cash into an accounting practice.*

Balances introduced by a double-entry system will prevent transactions that could be overlooked in a single-entry system.

Do I need to do something with owner's equity?   Where should I put office equipment?

Invested office equipment and cash into an accounting practice.

Single-entry system cash is recorded in the checkbook. The entry would include an increase to capital under owner's equity.

Steps in a Double-Entry Accounting System

Step 1: Identify key words in a transaction.
Invested office equipment and **cash** into an accounting practice.

Step 2: Identify at least two accounts that are affected.

Capital ◄   In this transaction,
Office equipment ◄   three accounts
Cash ◄   were affected.

Step 3: Classify those accounts as to assets, liabilities, owner's equity, revenue or expenses.

Assets   **Owner's Equity**
Cash   Capital
Office Equipment

Step 4: Increase or decrease the accounts.

+ Capital
+ Office Equipment
+ Cash

Step 5: Record the entry.

The double-entry system is like a teeter totter. After each transaction the teeter totter must remain in balance.

Example: *Invested $4,000 office equipment and $10,000 cash into an accounting practice.*

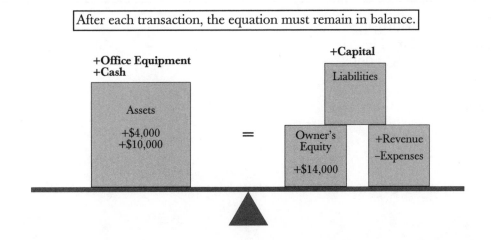

Examples of the Double-Entry Accounting System

The following are some examples of business transactions. Remember the basic rules of every business transaction in a double-entry account system.

Basic Rules: At least two accounts must be used. The Balance Sheet equation must remain in balance after every transaction.

1. The company started with an investment of $50,000.

Assets	=	Liabilities	+	Owner's Equity	Revenue	–	Expenses
Cash +$50,000				Capital +$50,000			

2. The company earned $20,000 on account.

Assets	=	Liabilities	+	Owner's Equity	Revenue	–	Expenses
Accounts/ Receivable + $20,000					Earnings + $20,000		

3. The company purchased a $55,000 building with $5,000 cash and a mortgage for the remainder.

Assets	=	Liabilities	+	Owner's Equity	Revenue	–	Expenses
Cash – $5,000		Mortgage/ Payable + $50,000					
Building + $55,000							

4. Paid $125 for the utilities bill.

Assets	=	Liabilities	+	Owner's Equity	Revenue	–	Expenses
Cash –$125							Utilities Expense –$125

5. Paid personal* telephone bill for $55.

Assets	=	Liabilities	+	Owner's Equity	Revenue	–	Expenses
Cash – $55				Withdrawal – $55			

The word personal makes this a withdrawal from the owner's capital resources, rather than an expense to the company.

A Few Recordkeeping Techniques

Dollar Signs These are not used in journals or ledgers.
Dollar signs should be placed on financial reports.
200

Commas Commas to show thousands of dollars are not
required in journals or ledgers.
1000

Decimal Points Decimal points are not required on ruled paper.
We will not use cents in many of the problems.
4000 | 00

Omission of Zeros You may use a dash to indicate zeros on problems.
5000–

Review

It is important to keep good records. They will help in managing the business, and provide good tax information for the Internal Revenue Service. A good chart of accounts will provide information to compare from accounting period to accounting period. This information can tell a story of how your business is doing, on a line item basis. Many businesses do not need a complicated set of books. Even if the only accounting system you are using is a checkbook, look at your entry a week from when you placed it in the book. If you cannot explain it, you have not recorded it properly.

Ledger and Journal

The Ledger

Each business transaction is recorded in the journal, then posted (placed) into the ledger book.

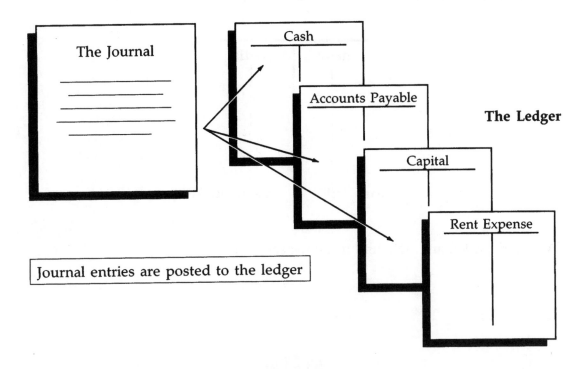

Journal entries are posted to the ledger

The ledger has all the accounts listed in order, beginning with assets, liabilities, owner's equity, revenue, and expense accounts. The general methods of recording these ledger account transactions are:

➤ After reading the transaction, determine which of the accounts are affected. In a double-entry accounting system, at least two accounts must be affected.

➤ Determine whether the accounts you selected are assets, liabilities, owner's equity, revenue, or expense.

➤ Determine if the accounts are increased or decreased by the transaction.

➤ Place the correct amount on the proper side of the "T" account to reflect the increase or decrease.

Debits and Credits in the Ledger Accounts

For hundreds of years, accountants have used the terms *debit* and *credit* when referring to placing numbers in the ledger books and Journals. This accounting jargon continues to confuse many people. The mystery is easy to solve:

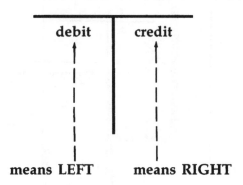

We could use left and right and mean the same thing.

Plus and Minus

The increase and decrease of an account is difficult to understand. The balance sheet equation helps:

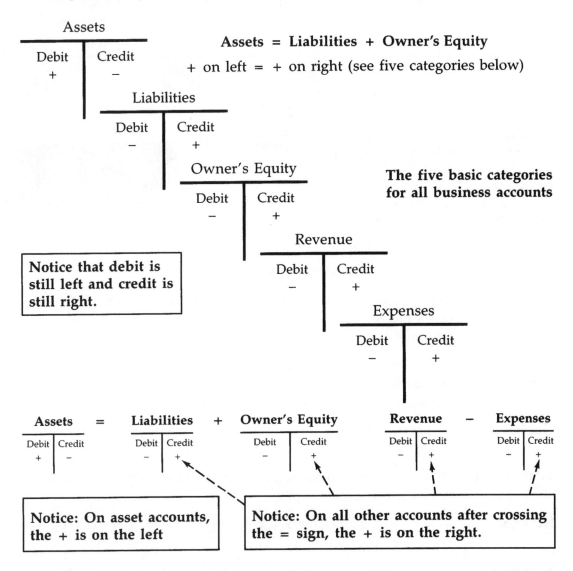

Assets = Liabilities + Owner's Equity

+ on left = + on right (see five categories below)

The five basic categories for all business accounts

Notice that debit is still left and credit is still right.

Notice: On asset accounts, the + is on the left

Notice: On all other accounts after crossing the = sign, the + is on the right.

Under expenses you will see that the debit (left side) has a minus. This means that a debit to an expense account decreases owner's equity—an increase to the expense account is a debit.

Example: If $60 has been expended in a gas expense account this would be a debit. If $40 more is added to this account the increase to the account is a debit but this expense account decreases equity.

Ledger Accounts

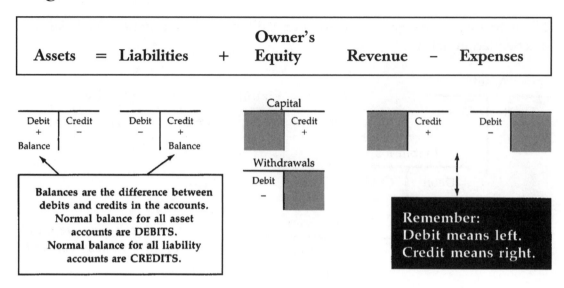

General Rules

Assets
When placing amounts in the asset accounts, you can debit and credit the account. However, the normal balance of all asset accounts at the end of the accounting period is a debit.

Liabilities
When placing amounts in the liability accounts, you can debit and credit the account; however, the normal balance of all liabilities accounts, at the end of the accounting period, is a credit.

Capital
When placing amounts in the capital account, you can only credit the account.

Withdrawals
When placing amounts in the withdrawal account, you can only debit the account.

Revenue
When placing amounts in the revenue account, you can only credit the accounts.

Expenses
When placing amounts in the expense account, you can only debit the accounts.

The 'T' Account

Below is the standard ledger account. The name comes from the "T" form, with debits to the left and credits to the right.

The Standard Ledger Account — "T" Account

Cash   **Account No. 101**

Date (Year)		Item	PR	Debit	Date (Year)		Item	PR	Credit
Jan	1		J1	2500	Jan	2		J1	250
					Jan	3		J1	175
				2500					425
		balance 2075							

The ending balance is the difference between the footings.

Footings help balance the account (to foot means to add).

Another Type of Standard Ledger Account

Account number. Every ledger account has a name and number.

Post reference. Used to record where the entry came from (Journal, page 1).

Cash   **Account No. 101**

Date (Year)		Explanation	PR	Debit	Credit	Balance
Jan	1		J1	2500		2500
	2		J1		250	2250
	3		J1		175	2075

This is not used much if you have a journal. Explanations are recorded in the Journal. Anything unusual will be written here.

Some T accounts use a balance column much the same as your checkbook.

THE LEDGER (CONTINUED)

Examples of Standard Ledger Accounts

On January 1, J.D. Smith of J.D. Services invested $5,000 cash and $100 office equipment.

Cash		Office Equipment		Capital	
Debit	Credit	Debit	Credit	Debit	Credit
5000		100			5100

On January 15, J.D. Services purchased a used truck for $1,000 cash and a note payable for $4,000.

Cash		Truck		Note Payable	
Debit	Credit	Debit	Credit	Debit	Credit
5000	1000	5000			4000

On January 17, J.D. Services earned $2,000 cash for cleaning services.

Cash		Revenue	
Debit	Credit	Debit	Credit
5000	1000		2000
2000			

On January 20, J.D. Services paid utilities on building for $200.

Cash		Utilities Expense	
Debit	Credit	Debit	Credit
5000	1000	200	
2000	200		

On January 21, J.D. Services paid the monthly rent for the building, $500.

Cash		Rent Expense	
Debit	Credit	Debit	Credit
5000	1000	500	
2000	200		
	500		

On January 22, J.D. Services purchased office supplies for $250.

Cash		Office Supplies	
Debit	Credit	Debit	Credit
5000	1000	250	
2000	200		
	500		
	250		

On January 24, J.D. Services withdrew $100 cash to pay personal expenses.

Cash		J. D. Withdrawals	
Debit	Credit	Debit	Credit
5000	1000	100	
2000	200		
	500		
	250		
	100		

Summary of J.D. Services Transactions

Cash		Note Payable	J. D. Capital
5000	1000	4000	
2000	200		5100
	500		
	250		
Balance	100		
4950			

Office Supplies		J.D. Withdrawals	
250		100	

Office Equipment		Revenue	
100			2000

Truck		Utilities Expense	
5000		200	

Wage Expense	
500	

The Trial Balance

The trial balance is prepared from the general ledger, at the end of the accounting period. Each account balance is recorded, and the totals for the debits and credits are compared. The two totals should equal each other. This does not mean an error was not made on the trial balance, but at least the debits equaled the credits at the end of the period.

J. D. Services Trial Balance December 31, (Year)		
	Debit	Credit
Cash	$4,950	
Office supplies	250	
Office equipment	100	
Truck	5,000	
Note Payable		$4,000
J. D. Capital		5,100
J. D. Withdrawals	100	
Revenue		2,000
Utilities Expense	200	
Rent Expense	500	
Totals	$11,100	$11,100

The trial balance is a listing of the ledger accounts in order, starting with assets, liabilities, owner's equity, revenue, and expenses.

Debits = Credits

Reviewing Ledger Accounts

ASSETS

Cash

Debit + Balance	Credit −

Accounts Receivable

+ Balance	−

Equipment

+ Balance	−

LIABILITIES

Accounts Payable

Debit −	Credit + Balance

Notes Payable

−	+ Balance

OWNER'S EQUITY

J. D. Capital

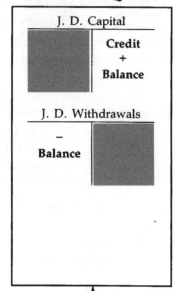

	Credit + Balance

J. D. Withdrawals

− Balance	

INCOME STATEMENT

Revenue

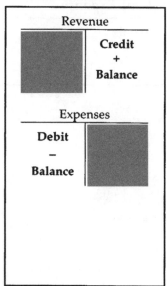

	Credit + Balance

Expenses

Debit − Balance	

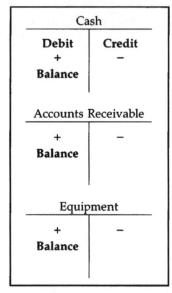

DEBIT MEANS LEFT.

CREDIT MEANS RIGHT.

This section on the ledger accounts is the most difficult to understand. If you need to review this, please do so before proceeding. Adjusting entries will be more confusing if you do not have a basic understanding of the double-entry system. Throughout this section, we have provided the basic rules. Many of the accounts, such as revenue, can be both debited and credited; however, we want you to understand the basics before learning about the exceptions.

The Journal

Place the first transaction of the accounting cycle in the journal. The journal, or general journal, records all transactions in chronological order. Each entry should be made on a daily basis, according to the time and date they occur. The journal is called the *book of original entry*. This book records transactions–debits (left side), then credits (right side).

Example: *January 1, invested $20,000 in cash in the business. January 2, paid rent for the business, $600.*

The Journal   **Page**

Date (Year)		Account Titles	P.R.	Debit	Credit
Jan	1	Cash		20000	
		Capital			20000
		Invested in the business			
	2	Rent Expense		600	
		Cash			600

Indent credits

Explanations help in remembering transactions

Skip between entries

Used to post ledger account number after placing amount in the ledger

Remember: Journal entries require debits (left side), then credits (right side).

THE JOURNAL (CONTINUED)

When making entries to the journal, the debits come first, then the credits. To help you think about the transaction, "T" accounts can help.

Example: *January 1, invested $10,000 cash in a truck and the remainder with a note payable. The truck costs $22,000.*

Truck	Cash	Note Payable
22000	**10000**	**12000**
Plus (increase)	Minus (decrease)	Plus (increase)

General Journal **Page**

Date (Year)		Account Titles	P.R.	Debit	Credit
Jan	1	Truck		22000	
		Cash			10000
		Note Payable			12000
		Purchased a new truck			

Types of Journals

There are many kinds of journals that you can purchase to help in placing similar accounts together.

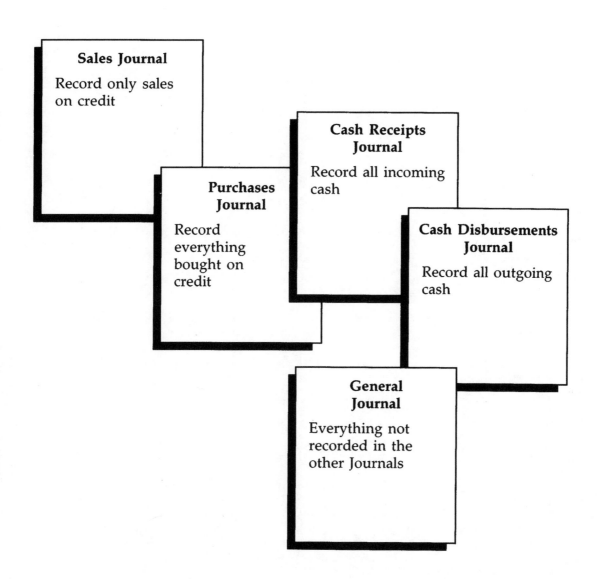

Sales Journal

Record only sales on credit

Purchases Journal

Record everything bought on credit

Cash Receipts Journal

Record all incoming cash

Cash Disbursements Journal

Record all outgoing cash

General Journal

Everything not recorded in the other Journals

Adjusting Entries

48

General Rules for Adjusting Entries

➤ Adjusting entries are made at the end of the month or accounting period.

➤ Cash is never used in an adjusting entry.

➤ An expense or revenue account is used in every transaction. Expenses will normally be debits, and revenue accounts will be credits.

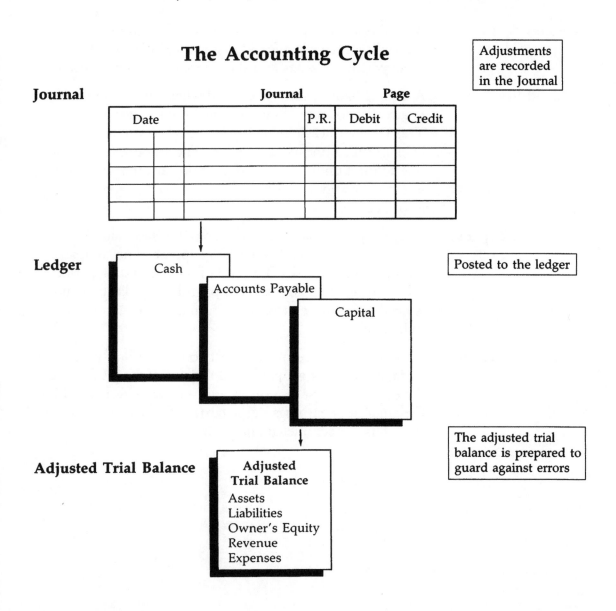

The Accounting Cycle

Journal

Adjustments are recorded in the Journal

Ledger

Posted to the ledger

Adjusted Trial Balance

The adjusted trial balance is prepared to guard against errors

Adjusting Entries

Once the accounting period entries and the trial balance have been completed, the accrual method requires adjusting entries to be made. Revenue and expense accounts that have been earned or used, but remain unrecorded, need to be adjusted.

There are four possible categories of adjusting entries identified from the Balance Sheet and Income Statement:

Assets
Accounts such as prepaid insurance, office supplies, and prepaid rent have been paid in advance. We recorded these prepayments as assets and should expense them as used.

Liabilities
A unique liability may be created when services are paid in advance for something the company has not done. This receipt of cash increases the cash account and a liability called unearned revenue. The amount remains in this account until it is earned. As you earn the amount in unearned revenue, it is transferred out of the account into revenue.

Accrued Expenses
These expenses have been incurred, but not paid. A good example of this would be payroll expense. The company pays every two weeks. The end of the accounting period arrives three days after the last payroll. An adjusting entry is needed for those three days, even though payroll is not to be paid.

Accrued Revenue
A job will not be completed for two months and your company will not get paid until the end of the project. At the end of the first month, an adjusting entry is needed for the amount of earnings in the current month, even though the job is not completed and no bill has been sent.

Adjusting Entries Overview

Accounts that need adjusting will be taken from the end of the period accounting cycle. Below is an overview of the kinds of accounts that need to be adjusted:

Trial Balance **ABC Company** **December 31, (Year)**
Cash Accounts Receivable
Prepaid Insurance **Office Supplies**
Equipment **Automobiles** **Buildings**
Land Accounts Payable Notes Payable
Unearned Revenue
Mortgage Payable Capital Withdrawals
Revenue
Wage Expense
Utilities Expense Repair Expense Advertising Expense

Assets need to be adjusted at the end of the accounting period. Prepaid insurance and office supplies are used during the period.

Depreciation is recorded on long-term assets. As assets are used over the accounting periods, the expense needs to be recorded on the income statement and reflected on the balance sheet.

Unearned revenue has been recorded when the business received cash for some service yet to be performed. This is a liability until it is performed.

Earnings not recorded at the end of the accounting period, but which have been partly completed.

ACCRUALS*

Expenses incurred, but not recorded.

Accruals are unpaid and unrecorded expenses and revenue.

Adjusting Current Assets

Current assets are adjusted by removing the used amount from the asset account and transferring it to the expense account. The adjusted trial balance below shows the result.

	Journal		P.R.	Debit	Credit
Date					
Dec	31	Office Supplies Exp		100	
		Office Supplies			100

Office supplies used during the accounting period

Adjusted Trial Balance

Cash	1000.00	
Accounts Receivable	5000.00	
Prepaid Insurance	600.00	
Office Supplies	400.00	
	300.00	
Equipment	10000.00	
Automobiles	24000.00	
Buildings	80000.00	
Land	25000.00	
Accounts Payable		25000.00
Notes Payable		15000.00
Unearned Revenue		1500.00
Mortgage Payable		80000.00
Capital		27500.00
Withdrawals	12000.00	
Revenue (earnings)		90000.00
Wage Expense	48000.00	
Office Supply Expense	**100.00**	
Utilities Expense	12000.00	
Repair Expense	6000.00	
Advertising Expense	15000.00	

Adjusting Entries for Long-Term Assets

Long-term assets need to be adjusted for the amount of depreciation (use) for the accounting period. An account called Accumulated Depreciation is used. This account is a contra-asset account (credit balance) instead of the normal debit balance of an asset. Over the accounting period, the book value will continue to decline as the accumulated depreciation account collects more of the used portion of the asset.

General Journal   Page

Date			P.R.	Debit	Credit
Dec	31	Depreciation Expense		2000	
		Accumulated Depr.			2000

Cash	1000.00	
Accounts Receivable	5000.00	The difference between the
Prepaid Insurance	600.00	cost and the depreciation is
Office Supplied	400.00	known as *book value*,
Equipment	10000.00	$8,000.
Accumulated Depreciation	2000.00	
Automobiles	24000.00	Book Value
Accumulated Depreciation	5000.00	$19,000.
Buildings	80000.00	Book Value
Accumulated Depreciation	4000.00	$76,000
Land	25000.00	
Accounts Payable		25000.00
Notes Payable		15000.00
Unearned Revenue		1500.00
Mortgage Payable		80000.00
Capital	12000.00	
Withdrawal		27500.00
Revenue (earnings)		90000.00
Wage Expense	48000.00	
Utilities Expense	12000.00	
Repair Expense	6000.00	
Advertising Expense	15000.00	
Depreciation Expense	2000.00	
Depreciation Expense	5000.00	Income Statement Expenses
Depreciation Expense	4000.00	

Long-Term Assets

Long-term assets need to be adjusted at the end of each accounting period. The adjustment is through depreciation, amortization, and depletion. A contra-asset account is used to keep the use separate from the asset account. The only exception to this case is the intangible assets, for which amortization is removed straight from the account.

Long-term assets include:

		Depreciation
Property:	Buildings	yes
	Land	no
Equipment:	Cars	yes
	Trucks	yes
	Office Equipment	yes
Land Improvements:	Parking lots	yes
	Sprinkler systems	yes
	Driveways	yes
Intangible Assets:	Patents	yes*
	Copyrights	yes*
	Franchises	yes*

> No contra account. Usage comes out of the account as a credit.

*This is called **amortization** instead of depreciation.

Natural Resources:	Oil	yes*
	Coal	yes*
	Timber	yes*

*This is called **depletion** instead of depreciation.

There are two parts to all long-term assets:

Determining the cost   **Determining depreciation**

This text will not discuss either of these topics, for which you can get clear definitions from the IRS or basic accounting texts. For our purposes, we are interested in determining the adjusting entries. Cost and depreciation will be provided.

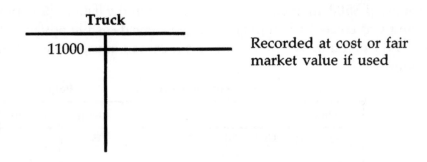

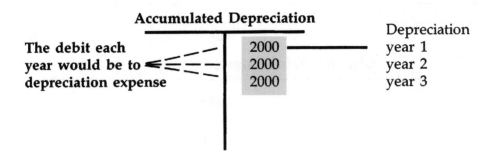

Depreciation and Book Value

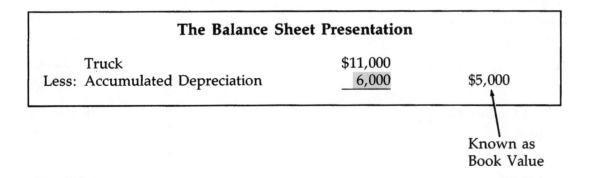

With this presentation, the business owner is reminded just how "old" the asset is getting and when it will be necessary to replace it.

Adjusting Current Liabilities

Earnings of $500 are recorded as revenue from the liability account. The liability account was created when the company received cash in advance, but had not earned the amount. When the amount is earned, it is transferred to the revenue account.

	General Journal		Page	

Date			P.R.	Debit	Credit
Dec	31	Unearned Revenue		500	
		Revenue			500

Adjusted Trial Balance

Cash	1000.00	
Accounts Receivable	5000.00	
Prepaid Insurance	600.00	
Office Supplies	400.00	
Equipment	10000.00	
Automobiles	24000.00	
Buildings	80000.00	
Land	25000.00	
Accounts Payable		25000.00
Notes Payable		15000.00
Unearned Revenue		~~1500.00~~
		1000.00
Mortgage Payable		80000.00
Capital		27500.00
Withdrawals	12000.00	
Revenue		~~90000.00~~
		90500.00
Wage Expense	48000.00	
Utilities Expense	12000.00	
Repair Expense	6000.00	
Advertising Expense	15000.00	

Adjusting Accrued Expense

This entry would be made by a company that pays the payroll on the 5th and 20th of the month. The last days of the month would be recorded as a payable, because the expense has been incurred, but the company will not make a payment until the 5th.

General Journal   Page

Date			P.R.	Debit	Credit
Dec	31	Wage Expense		1500	
		Wage Payable			1500

Adjusted Trial Balance

Cash	1000.00	
Accounts Receivable	5000.00	
Prepaid Insurance	600.00	
Office Supplies	400.00	
Equipment	10000.00	
Automobiles	24000.00	
Buildings	80000.00	
Land	25000.00	
Accounts Payable		25000.00
Wage Payable		**1500.00**
Notes Payable		15000.00
Unearned Payable		1500.00
Mortgage Payable		80000.00
Capital		27500.00
Withdrawals	12000.00	
Revenue		90000.00
Wage Expense	~~48000.00~~	
	49500.00	
Utilities Expense	12000.00	
Repair Expense	6000.00	
Advertising Expense	15000.00	

Adjusting Accrued Revenue

This entry is made for a job that is not completed by the end of the accounting period, but needs to be recorded since the service was performed in the accounting period.

General Journal   **Page**

Date			P.R.	Debit	Credit
Dec	31	Accounts Receivable		1000	
		Revenue			1000

Adjusted Trial Balance

Cash	1000.00	
Accounts Receivable	~~5000.00~~	
	6000.00	
Prepaid Insurance	600.00	
Office Supplies	400.00	
Equipment	10000.00	
Automobiles	24000.00	
Buildings	80000.00	
Land	25000.00	
Accounts Payable		25000.00
Notes Payable		15000.00
Unearned Revenue		1500.00
Mortgage Payable		80000.00
Capital		27500.00
Withdrawals	12000.00	
Revenue		~~90000.00~~
		91000.00
Wage Expense	48000.00	
Utilities Expense	12000.00	
Repair Expense	6000.00	
Advertising Expense	15000.00	

Basic Rules: *Adjusting Entries to Revenue*

There are only three ways to get revenue:

From cash **From an account receivable** (you did something and did not get paid) **From unearned revenue** (you were paid in advance for something you have not done)

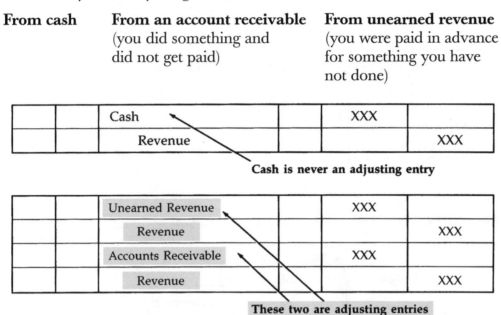

		Cash		XXX	
		Revenue			XXX

Cash is never an adjusting entry

		Unearned Revenue		XXX	
		Revenue			XXX
		Accounts Receivable		XXX	
		Revenue			XXX

These two are adjusting entries

Adjusting Entries to Expenses

There are only three ways to get expenses:

From cash **From an account payable** (you had an expense and did not pay) **From prepaid assets** (you paid in advance for something you have not used)

		Expense		XXX	
		Cash			XXX

Cash is never an adjusting entry

		Expense		XXX	
		Accounts Payable			XXX
		Insurance Expense		XXX	
		Prepaid Insurance			XXX

These two are adjusting entries

Review

Adjusting Entries

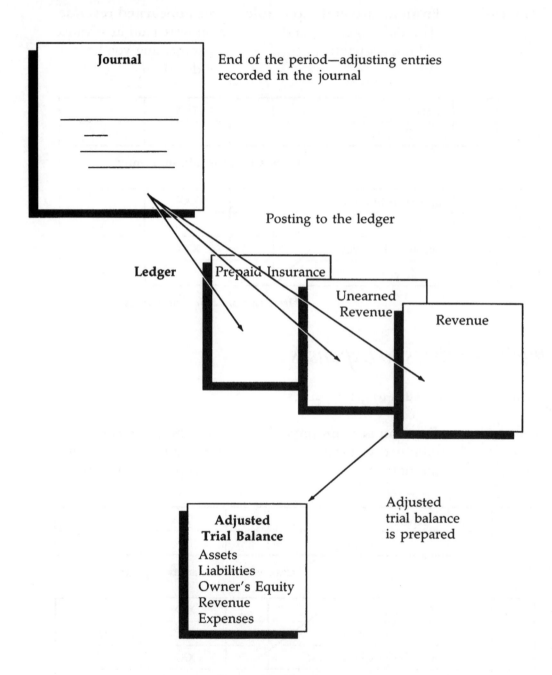

Journal

End of the period—adjusting entries recorded in the journal

Posting to the ledger

Ledger

Prepaid Insurance

Unearned Revenue

Revenue

Adjusted Trial Balance

Assets
Liabilities
Owner's Equity
Revenue
Expenses

Adjusted trial balance is prepared

Closing Entries

Closing Entries—An Overview

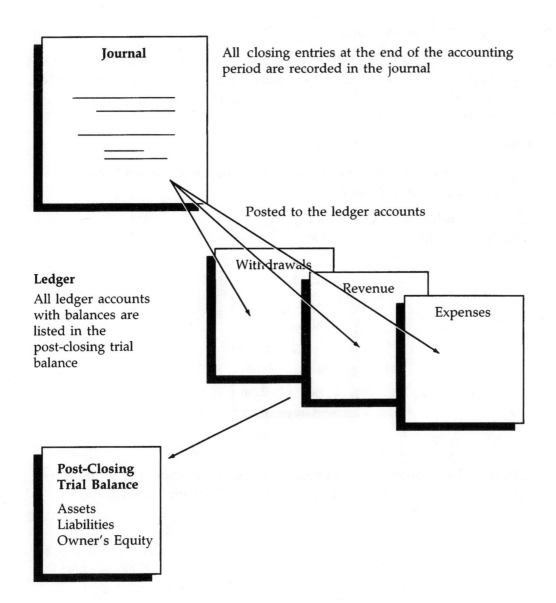

Journal

All closing entries at the end of the accounting period are recorded in the journal

Posted to the ledger accounts

Withdrawals

Revenue

Expenses

Ledger

All ledger accounts with balances are listed in the post-closing trial balance

Post-Closing Trial Balance

Assets
Liabilities
Owner's Equity

CLOSING ENTRIES (CONTINUED)

Why do we need to close accounts to zero?

At the end of each month, we close revenue, expense, and withdrawal accounts to zero to keep a month-by-month comparison of what was used or earned. This is an opportunity to analyze different accounting periods, without previous totals in the accounts.

Important to remember:

Closing entries move the difference between revenue and expenses from the Income Statement to owner's equity.

Assets = Liabilities + Owner's Equity
10,500   3,200   7,300

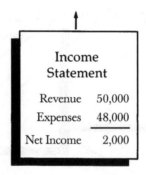

Income Statement	
Revenue	50,000
Expenses	48,000
Net Income	2,000

This Balance Sheet equation cannot balance without the amount of profit or loss from the Income Statement. This amount is moved through a closing entry.

Temporary and Permanent Accounts

Permanent accounts are on the Balance Sheet and temporary accounts are on the Income Statement.

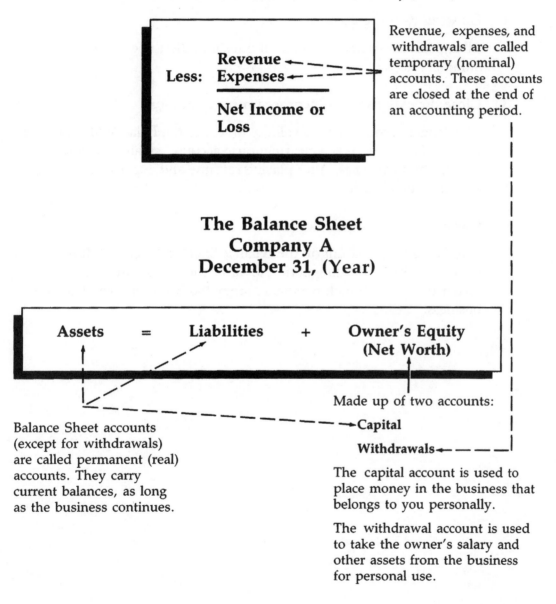

The Income Statement
For the Month Ended December 31, (Year)

Less: **Revenue**
Expenses

Net Income or Loss

Revenue, expenses, and withdrawals are called temporary (nominal) accounts. These accounts are closed at the end of an accounting period.

The Balance Sheet
Company A
December 31, (Year)

Assets   =   Liabilities   +   Owner's Equity (Net Worth)

Balance Sheet accounts (except for withdrawals) are called permanent (real) accounts. They carry current balances, as long as the business continues.

Made up of two accounts:

→**Capital**

Withdrawals◄— — — —

The capital account is used to place money in the business that belongs to you personally.

The withdrawal account is used to take the owner's salary and other assets from the business for personal use.

The Four Basic Entries to Closing Accounts

1. **Close all revenue accounts.**

   All revenue accounts need to start over at the end of each month. We cannot erase the balance in this account at the end of the month. The account is closed to the Expense and Income Summary (or just Income Summary).

2. **Close all expense accounts.**

   All expense accounts are closed at once into the Expense and Income Summary account.

3. **Close the expense and income summary account.**

   This ledger account has no validity on either the Balance Sheet or the Income Statement. It is a clearinghouse account, created to close revenue and expenses. After placing revenue and expense in the account, you close it.

4. **Close the withdrawal account.**

   This is the only account on the Balance Sheet to be closed. It is done at the end of the accounting period to allow the banker, investors or owner to see how much personal money has been removed from the business.

Closing Entries Illustrated

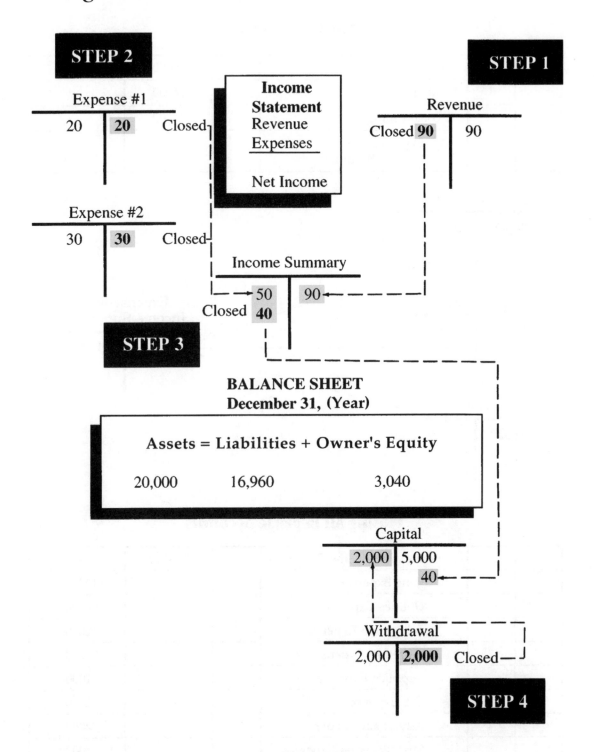

CLOSING ENTRIES ILLUSTRATED (CONTINUED)

Closing Revenue

		Tax Returns		10000	
		Consulting		36000	
		Recordkeeping		24000	
		Expense and Income Summary			70000

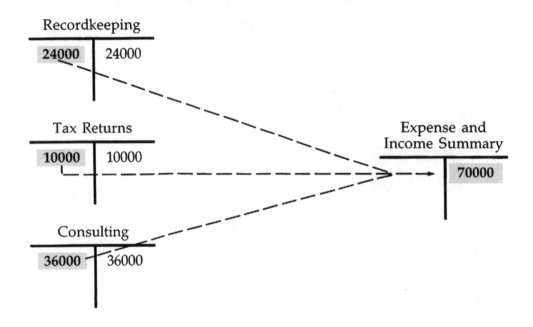

Closing All Expense Accounts

		Expense and Income Summary		108000	
		Rent Expense			12000
		Utilities Expense			60000
		Telephone Expense			12000
		Secretary Expense			18000
		Supplies Expense			1000
		Car Expense			2000
		Advertising Expense			2000
		Miscellaneous Expense			1000

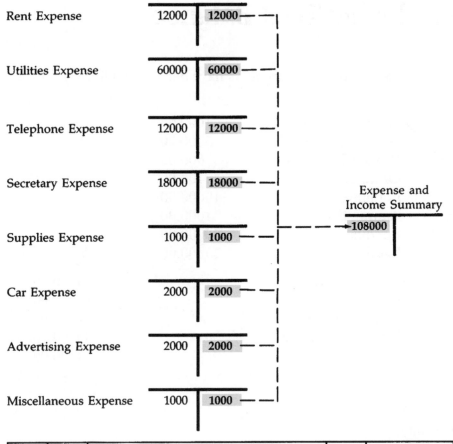

		Capital		38000	
		Expense and Income Summary			38000
		Capital		24000	
		Withdrawals			24000

Expenses are greater than revenue.
Closing the account requires the
credit for $38,000. If expenses had
been less than revenue, the
closing entry would be a debit.

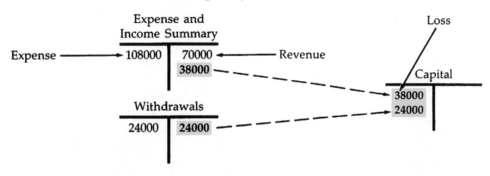

The Post-Closing Trial Balance

The revenue, expense, and withdrawal accounts have been closed to zero for the next accounting period.

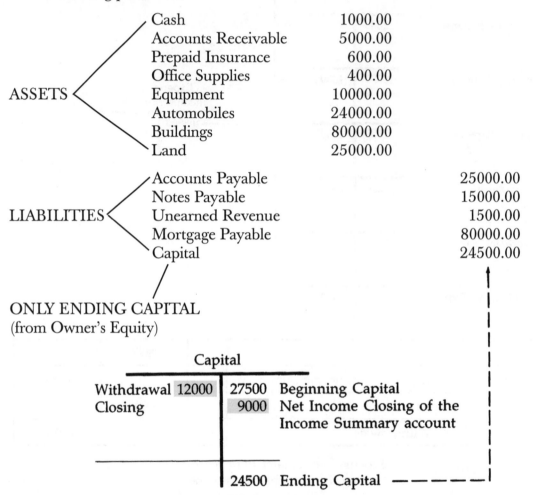

ASSETS	Cash	1000.00
	Accounts Receivable	5000.00
	Prepaid Insurance	600.00
	Office Supplies	400.00
	Equipment	10000.00
	Automobiles	24000.00
	Buildings	80000.00
	Land	25000.00

LIABILITIES	Accounts Payable	25000.00
	Notes Payable	15000.00
	Unearned Revenue	1500.00
	Mortgage Payable	80000.00
	Capital	24500.00

ONLY ENDING CAPITAL
(from Owner's Equity)

Capital

Withdrawal 12000	27500 Beginning Capital
Closing	9000 Net Income Closing of the Income Summary account
	24500 Ending Capital

The Four Steps to Closing Entries

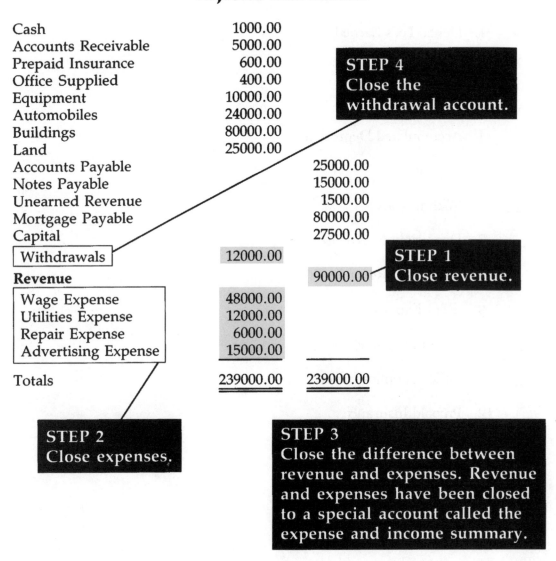

Adjusted Trial Balance

Cash	1000.00	
Accounts Receivable	5000.00	
Prepaid Insurance	600.00	
Office Supplied	400.00	
Equipment	10000.00	
Automobiles	24000.00	
Buildings	80000.00	
Land	25000.00	
Accounts Payable		25000.00
Notes Payable		15000.00
Unearned Revenue		1500.00
Mortgage Payable		80000.00
Capital		27500.00
Withdrawals	12000.00	
Revenue		90000.00
Wage Expense	48000.00	
Utilities Expense	12000.00	
Repair Expense	6000.00	
Advertising Expense	15000.00	
Totals	239000.00	239000.00

STEP 4
Close the
withdrawal account.

STEP 1
Close revenue.

STEP 2
Close expenses.

STEP 3
Close the difference between
revenue and expenses. Revenue
and expenses have been closed
to a special account called the
expense and income summary.

SELF-TEST 3: CLOSING ACCOUNTS

Identify the accounts to be closed. Place a **"C"** next to the accounts that should be closed and an **"X"** next to the accounts not closed.

___ 1. Dental Fees Earned

___ 2. Cash

___ 3. Wage Expense

___ 4. Accumulated Depreciation

___ 5. Capital

___ 6. Withdrawals

___ 7. Depreciation Expense

___ 8. Unearned Revenue

___ 9. Rent Expense

___ 10. Salaries Payable

___ 11. Office Supplies Expense

___ 12. Prepaid Insurance

___ 13. Interest Expense

___ 14. Interest Payable

___ 15. Interest Earned

If you have any problems with the solutions to this self-test, please review the previous sections.

Check your answers with the author's solutions in the Appendix.

Self-Test 4: Closings/Post-Closing Trial Balance

Identify the accounts that would appear on the post-closing trial balance. Place an **"A"** next to each account that would appear and an **"X"** by each account that would not appear.

___ 1. Capital

___ 2. Accounts Receivable

___ 3. Withdrawals

___ 4. Unearned Revenue

___ 5. Accounts Payable

___ 6. Depreciation Expense

___ 7. Wages Payable

___ 8. Wages Expense

___ 9. Accumulated Depreciation

___ 10. Office Equipment

___ 11. Revenue

___ 12. Rent Expense

___ 13. Income Summary

___ 14. Prepaid Insurance

___ 15. Interest Payable

If you have any problems with the solutions to this self-test, please review the previous sections.

Check your answers with the author's solutions in the Appendix.

Review

Closing entries can be very confusing if you did not learn the basics in the section on ledger accounts. Remember: there are temporary and permanent accounts. The temporary accounts need to be closed out at the end of each accounting period so the business can start with accounts in zero balance.

There are four basic closing entries:

➤ Close revenue

➤ Close expenses

➤ Close the income summary

➤ Close withdrawals

A post-closing trial balance is used to verify that the accounts are closed.

The Balance Sheet
and
Income Statement

Preparation of the Financial Statements

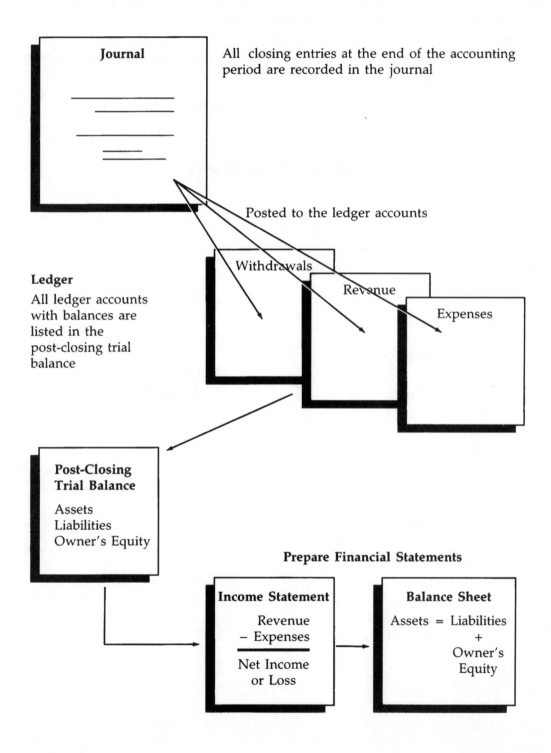

Journal

All closing entries at the end of the accounting period are recorded in the journal

Posted to the ledger accounts

Withdrawals

Revenue

Expenses

Ledger

All ledger accounts with balances are listed in the post-closing trial balance

Post-Closing Trial Balance

Assets
Liabilities
Owner's Equity

Prepare Financial Statements

Income Statement

Revenue
– Expenses
_____
Net Income
or Loss

Balance Sheet

Assets = Liabilities
+
Owner's
Equity

The Balance Sheet and Income Statement

The Balance Sheet can be prepared after the end-of-the-month adjusting entries have been entered in the journal and ledger, and the adjusted trial balance has been prepared. The closing entries listed above are not required to complete the Balance Sheet or the Income Statement. If desired, statements can be the last task of the accounting period.

The Income Statement accounts are listed at the bottom of the adjusted trial balance, starting with revenue.

The Adjusted Trial Balance

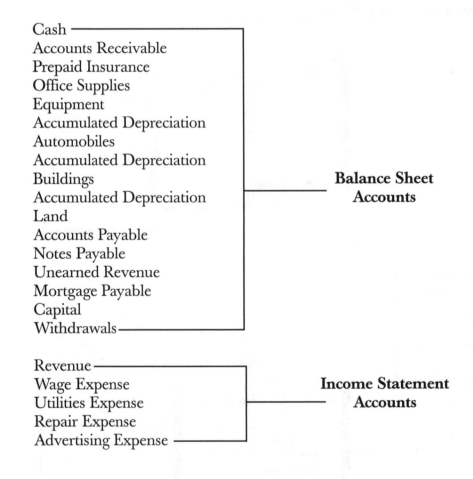

Cash
Accounts Receivable
Prepaid Insurance
Office Supplies
Equipment
Accumulated Depreciation
Automobiles
Accumulated Depreciation
Buildings
Accumulated Depreciation
Land
Accounts Payable
Notes Payable
Unearned Revenue
Mortgage Payable
Capital
Withdrawals

**Balance Sheet
Accounts**

Revenue
Wage Expense
Utilities Expense
Repair Expense
Advertising Expense

**Income Statement
Accounts**

Reviewing the Balance Sheet and Income Statement

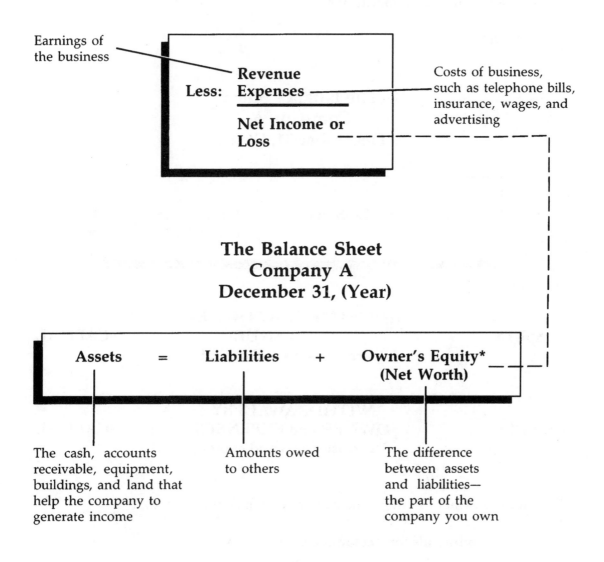

The Income Statement
For the Month Ended December 31, (Year)

Earnings of
the business

Revenue

Less: **Expenses**

**Net Income or
Loss**

Costs of business,
such as telephone bills,
insurance, wages, and
advertising

The Balance Sheet
Company A
December 31, (Year)

Assets   =   Liabilities   +   Owner's Equity*
(Net Worth)

The cash, accounts
receivable, equipment,
buildings, and land that
help the company to
generate income

Amounts owed
to others

The difference
between assets
and liabilities—
the part of the
company you own

---

*The Balance Sheet equation cannot balance until net income or loss is added to the Balance Sheet from the Income Statement. The movement of this profit or loss is completed through closing entries (see Part 6).

The Balance Sheet

The business owner can make the company grow in three ways:

➢ **Investment of personal cash or assets**

➢ **Revenue from operations**

➢ **Debt**

**The Balance Sheet
Company A
December 31, (Year)**

| Assets | = | Liabilities | + | Owner's Equity (Net Worth) |

+ASSETS   **INVESTMENT BY OWNER and REVENUE** (Increase assets and capital)   **+CAPITAL**

–ASSETS   **WITHDRAWALS BY OWNER and EXPENSES** (Decrease assets and capital)   **–CAPITAL**

The business owner can make the company decline in three ways:

➢ **Withdrawals for personal cash or assets**

➢ **Expenses from operations**

➢ **Too much debt**

Classifying the Balance Sheet

Assets

Current Assets:
  Cash
  Marketable Securities
  Accounts Receivable
  Prepaid Expenses

Assets received or consumed within one year or within the operating cycle, whichever is longer

Long-Term Investments:
  Investments
  Bonds

Stocks and bonds that will be held more than one year or one cycle

Plant and Equipment:
  Machinery and Equipment
  Buildings
  Land

Long-term assets, expected to last more than one year or one operating cycle

Intangibles:
  Copyrights
  Patents
  Franchises

Assets having no physical properties

Other Assets:
  Security Deposits
  Receivables from corporate officers

Assets of more than one year or one operating cycle, that do not fit into any other category

Liabilities

Current Liabilities:
  Account payable
  Notes payable
  Wages payable

Liabilities incurred and due within one year or within the operating cycle, whichever is longer

Long-Term Liabilities:
  Mortgage payable
  Notes payable

Long-term liabilities expected to be incurred longer than one year or one operating cycle

Owner's Equity

Capital

The Income Statement

Expense Accounts for the Income Statement

The Internal Revenue Service Federal Tax Return Schedule "C" Part II provides a list of expense accounts used by sole proprietorships. If you have trouble coming up with your own list, start with what the IRS provides you.

Part II	Expenses. Enter expenses for business use of your home **only** on line 30.				
8	Advertising	8	19	Pension and profit-sharing plans	19
9	Bad debts from sales or services (see page C-3)	9	20	Rent or lease (see page C-4):	
			a	Vehicles, machinery, and equipment	20a
10	Car and truck expenses (see page C-3)	10	b	Other business property	20b
			21	Repairs and maintenance	21
11	Commissions and fees	11	22	Supplies (not included in Part III)	22
12	Depletion	12	23	Taxes and licenses	23
13	Depreciation and section 179 expense deduction (not included in Part III) (see page C-3)	13	24	Travel, meals, and entertainment:	
			a	Travel	24a
14	Employee benefit programs (other than on line 19)	14	b	Meals and entertainment	
15	Insurance (other than health)	15	c	Enter nondeductible amount included on line 24b (see page C-5)	
16	Interest:				
a	Mortgage (paid to banks, etc.)	16a	d	Subtract line 24c from line 24b	24d
b	Other	16b	25	Utilities	25
17	Legal and professional services	17	26	Wages (less employment credits)	26
18	Office expense	18	27	Other expenses (from line 48 on page 2)	27
28	Total expenses before expenses for business use of home. Add lines 8 through 27 in columns ▶				28
29	Tentative profit (loss). Subtract line 28 from line 7				29
30	Expenses for business use of your home. Attach **Form 8829**				30
31	**Net profit or (loss).** Subtract line 30 from line 29.				
	• If a profit, enter on **Form 1040, line 12,** and **also** on **Schedule SE, line 2** (statutory employees, see page C-5). Estates and trusts, enter on Form 1041, line 3.				31
	• If a loss, you **must** go on to line 32.				
32	If you have a loss, check the box that describes your investment in this activity (see page C-5).				
	• If you checked 32a, enter the loss on **Form 1040, line 12,** and **also** on **Schedule SE, line 2** (statutory employees, see page C-5). Estates and trusts, enter on Form 1041, line 3.		32a ☐	All investment is at risk.	
	• If you checked 32b, you **must** attach **Form 6198.**		32b ☐	Some investment is not at risk.	

For Paperwork Reduction Act Notice, see Form 1040 instructions.
ISA
STF FED2615F.1

Schedule C (Form 1040) 2000

Sample Income Statement and Balance Sheet

J. D. Repair Shop
Income Statement
For the Month Ended Jan. 31, (Year)

REVENUE:		
Electronic Repair Income (Revenue)		$16,520
Interest Income		250
Total Revenue		$16,770
EXPENSES:		
Rent Expense	$ 1,500	
Utilities Expense	900	
Supplies Expense	4,000	
Wage Expense	10,000	
Total Expenses		16,400
NET INCOME (LOSS)		$ 370

J. D. Repair Shop
Balance Sheet
January 31, (Year)

ASSETS		LIABILITIES	
Cash	$ 670	Accounts Payable	$ 500
Accounts Receivable	3,500	Notes Payable	1,000
Supplies	2,500	Total Liabilities	$1,500
		OWNER'S EQUITY	
		J. D. Capital	$5,000
		Net Income	370
		Less Withdrawals	200
		J. D. Capital (ending)	5,170
	$6,670		$6,670

Note: The Balance Sheet cannot balance until the net profit of $370 is brought into the equity section of the Balance Sheet.

SELF-TEST 5: IDENTIFY THE FINANCIAL STATEMENT ACCOUNTS

Identify the accounts. Place the appropriate letter next to each account:

A = Assets
L = Liabilities
OE = Owner's Equity
R = Revenue
E = Expense

Example:
_____A_____ Prepaid Insurance

1. _____ Cash

2. _____ Prepaid Rent

3. _____ Accounts Payable

4. _____ Supplies Used

5. _____ Investments

6. _____ Notes Payable

7. _____ Supplies

8. _____ Capital

9. _____ Equipment

10. _____ Wage Expense

11. _____ Withdrawal

12. _____ Utilities Expense

13. _____ Buildings

14. _____ Wage Payable

15. _____ Land

If you have any problems with the solutions to this self-test, please review the previous sections.

Check your answers with the author's solutions in the Appendix.

SELF-TEST 6: IDENTIFY STATEMENTS

Place an **"X"** for the normal balance in the appropriate column for each account. Use no more than one **"X"** per account. Each account can be on only one statement.

	Income Statement		Balance Sheet	
	Debit	Credit	Debit	Credit
1. Accounts Payable				
2. Capital				
3. Cash				
4. Salaries Payable				
5. Prepaid Insurance				
6. Dental Fees				
7. Accounts Receivable				
8. Telephone Expense				
9. Withdrawals				
10. Land				
11. Salary Expense				
12. Office Supplies				
13. Notes Payable				
14. Interest Payable				

If you have any problems with the solutions to this self-test, please review the previous sections.

Check your answers with the author's solutions in the Appendix.

SELF-TEST 7: CLASSIFYING BALANCE SHEET ACCOUNTS

Identify the accounts. Place the letter next to the accounts.

A = Current Assets
B = Long-Term Investments
C = Plant and Equipment
D = Intangible Assets
E = Current Liabilities

F = Long-Term Liabilities
G = Owner's Equity
H = Revenue
I = Expenses

1. _____ Salaries Payable

2. _____ Capital

3. _____ Mortgage Payable

4. _____ Parking Lot

5. _____ Accounts Receivable

6. _____ Note Receivable (two years)

7. _____ Land

8. _____ Invested in Long-Term Bonds

9. _____ Withdrawals

10. _____ Wages Earned by Employees

11. _____ Note Payable (due in two weeks)

If you have any problems with the solutions to this self-test, please review the previous sections.

Check your answers with the author's solutions in the Appendix.

Review

The Balance Sheet and the Income Statement provide the two basic statements for financial reporting. Income Statements should be prepared on a monthly basis. Many small firms do not keep track of items on that basis, and each month critical information on the flow of sales and expenses is lost.

There are other statements of equal importance in the accounting cycle. One such report is a cash-in and cash-out statement that reports the flow of cash through the business. This statement is most critical where a company has accounts receivable. Cash is the life blood of the business. Your business can be doing well and not survive because of cash flow problems.

Remember, information is necessary to analyze how you are doing. Good recordkeeping and statement comparisons will provide a detailed map that identifies where you have been and where you can go.

Special
Consideration:
Inventory

The Basic Difference of a Merchandise Company

The primary purpose of the merchandise store is to sell goods, rather than services. Merchandise companies may be wholesale operations that sell to retailers, or retailer operations that sell to the consumer.

This purchase of merchandise adds an entire new statement to the Income Statement, called *cost of goods sold.*

Merchandise Company   **Service Company**

The Income Statement		The Income Statement	
	Sales		Sales
Less:	**Cost of Goods Sold**	Less:	Expenses
=	Gross Profit	=	Net Income
Less:	Expenses		
=	Net Income		

	Sales	$500		Sales	$500
Less:	**Cost of Goods Sold**	250	Less:	Expenses	100
=	Gross Profit	$250	=	Net Income	$400
Less:	Expenses	100			
=	Net Income	$150			

Decisions About Inventory

What Inventory System Will You Use?

Perpetual or Periodic

Perpetual inventory systems keep continuous records of the cost and amount of inventory on hand and what has been sold at the time of sale.

Periodic inventory is the amount of inventory or cost of goods sold that cannot be found on a continuous basis. The inventory must be counted, and the cost of goods sold must be computed.

How Will You Cost Inventory?*

Cost or Lower of Cost or Market

Cost of inventory is the price of the inventory at the time of purchase. If the cost method is used to determine price, the market will have no bearing on the decision.

Lower of cost or market can be used when a decline in price of inventory falls below the original cost. Market price is then used to value inventory instead of cost. If market price goes back higher than cost, cost will be used to determine inventory.

---

*Inventory methods, once selected, cannot be changed without IRS approval.

What Type of Inventory Flow Will You Use?

Specific Invoice

This method requires that each unit of inventory be tagged so the cost of each one can be determined at the time of inventory count.

Weighted Average

This method of inventory flow takes the number of units purchased and the total cost of all purchases. When you divide the cost by the number of units purchased, the result is a weighted average.

$400 $400 $450 $450 $500

$$\frac{\$2,200}{5} = \$440 \text{ per bike}$$

If two bikes are left in inventory, the weighted average is $880.

DECISIONS ABOUT INVENTORY(CONTINUED)

First-in, First-out

Ending inventory is assigned costs as a result of the most recent purchases. First-in, first-out refers to the items sold, not to the items in inventory.

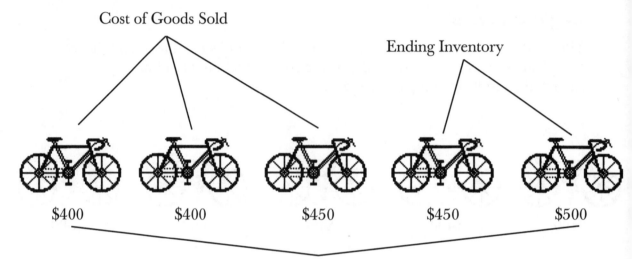

Cost of Goods Sold

Ending Inventory

$400 $400 $450 $450 $500

Goods Available to Sell

Last-in, First-out

Ending inventory is assigned costs as a result of the beginning inventory and earliest purchases. Last-in, first-out refers to the items sold, not to the items in inventory.

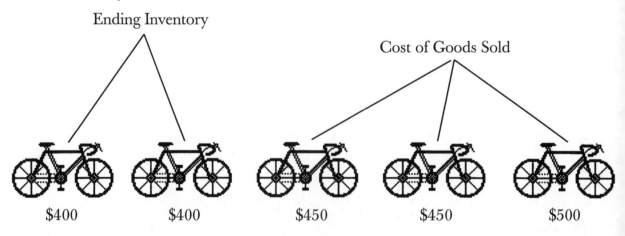

Ending Inventory

Cost of Goods Sold

$400 $400 $450 $450 $500

Comparison of Inventory Flow Methods

	Weighted Average	FIFO	LIFO
Goods Available for Sale (5 bikes)	$2,200	$2,200	$2,200
Less: Ending Inventory (2 bikes)	880	950	800
= Cost of Goods Sold	1,320	1,250	1,400

Sales were: $2,100 ($700 x 3)

	Weighted Average	FIFO	LIFO
Sales	$2,100	$2,100	$2,100
Less: Cost of Goods Sold	1,320	1,250	1,400
Gross Profit	$780	$850	$700

Which method would you choose?*

➤ LIFO gives the lowest gross profit, therefore, the lowest tax on profit.

➤ In general, when the purchase price of inventory is going down, choose FIFO.

➤ When the purchase price of inventory is going up, choose LIFO.

➤ When it goes up and down, choose weighted average.

*Inventory methods, once selected, cannot be changed without IRS approval.

Review

Inventory is complicated. We have given you some of the basic questions and answers of where and how your business needs to cost and flow inventory. The more dollars that are tied up in this account on your Balance Sheet, the more information and help you should acquire on tax preparation. You can save substantial dollars by managing your inventory well.

JD TeeShirts
Balance Sheet
December 31, 2000

Current Assets:	
Cash	$ 2,000
Accounts Receivable	5,500
Inventory	**10,000**

Remember a business needs to keep enough inventory on hand to meet the needs of its customers. At the same time, too much inventory increases the risk of insolvency by: tying up cash; risk of price declines; damage; or loss of customer demand.

It is a good practice to use established measures of inventory effectiveness and efficiency using financial calculations such as: inventory turnover and number of days' sales in inventory.

Business Decisions

Introduction

We have included this short section on business decisions because the decisions here can change the accounting system and chart of accounts used by your business. A manufacturer needs to be concerned with cost accounting and inventory far more than a service company.

The business form—sole proprietorship, partnership, or corporation—will influence the tax forms used, as well as the chart of accounts. Keeping the proper records can provide your business with the audit trail it needs for good information.

Types of Business

As a new business, the accounts you will use are determined by the type of business you have. There are three distinct groups of businesses:

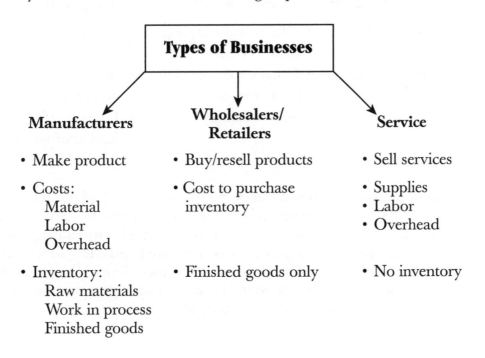

Types of Businesses

Manufacturers	**Wholesalers/ Retailers**	**Service**
• Make product	• Buy/resell products	• Sell services
• Costs: 　Material 　Labor 　Overhead	• Cost to purchase 　inventory	• Supplies • Labor • Overhead
• Inventory: 　Raw materials 　Work in process 　Finished goods	• Finished goods only	• No inventory

Business Form

First you must decide what type of business you have. Then you must decide what form of business ownership you want to establish. This decision will affect your recordkeeping. Listed below are some of the reasons for establishing one of these types of businesses. There are many reasons why you might wish to become a corporation or partnership, or remain a sole proprietorship.

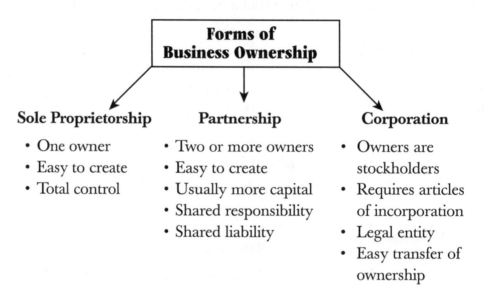

Forms of Business Ownership

Sole Proprietorship

- One owner
- Easy to create
- Total control

Partnership

- Two or more owners
- Easy to create
- Usually more capital
- Shared responsibility
- Shared liability

Corporation

- Owners are stockholders
- Requires articles of incorporation
- Legal entity
- Easy transfer of ownership

Many small businesses rush into corporation status, only to find out they could have waited. Small business owners have gone to the expense of starting as a corporation, only to go out of business in the first year. This was an expense they need not have incurred early in the business. We have listed a few strong points under each form. There are disadvantages to all of these forms. Your individual needs must be considered when deciding this issue. Please get more than one opinion if you are in doubt as to the relevancy of a form.

A Little Advice:

You can change your decision from a sole proprietorship to a corporation much more easily than you can from a corporation to a sole proprietorship.

A P P E N D I X

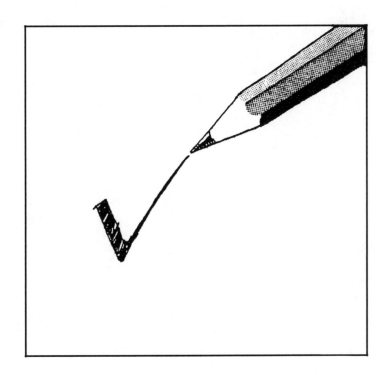

Solutions to the Self-Tests

Self-Test 1: Cash vs. Accrual Accounting (Page 17)

	Accrual Accounting	Cash Accounting
Revenue	$8,000	$3,500
Rent Expense	$1,000	$1,000
Wage Expense	1,200	600
Utilities Expense	300	300
Equipment Expense	500	—
Miscellaneous Expense	100	100
Office Supplies	200	—
Net Profit or (Loss)	$4,700	$1,500

Self-Test 2: Key Word Recognition (Page 24)

1. Performed <u>services</u> for a client for <u>cash</u>.

2. Performed <u>services</u> for a client <u>on account</u>.

3. <u>Paid</u> the secretaries' <u>wages</u>.

4. <u>Paid</u> the <u>utilities bill</u>.

5. Collected the <u>cash</u> <u>on the account</u> in transaction #2.

6. <u>Paid</u> a <u>three-year insurance</u> policy.

7. <u>Invested</u> <u>cash</u> in the business.

8. Performed <u>services</u> <u>on account</u>.

9. <u>Paid</u> the <u>telephone bill</u>.

10. Purchased <u>office equipment</u> for <u>cash</u> and the remainder <u>on account</u>.

Self-Test 3: Closing Accounts (Page 72)

  C   1. Dental Fees Earned

  X   2. Cash

  C   3. Wage Expense

  X   4. Accumulated Depreciation

  X   5. Capital

  C   6. Withdrawals

  C   7. Depreciation Expense

  X   8. Unearned Revenue

  C   9. Rent Expense

  X 10. Salaries Payable

  C 11. Office Supplies Expense

  X 12. Prepaid Insurance

  C 13. Interest Expense

  X 14. Interest Payable

  C 15. Interest Earned

Self-Test 4: Closings/Post-Closing Trial Balance (Page 73)

A   1.   Capital

A   2.   Accounts Receivable

X   3.   Withdrawals

A   4.   Unearned Revenue

A   5.   Accounts Payable

X   6.   Depreciation Expense

A   7.   Wages Payable

X   8.   Wages Expense

A   9.   Accumulated Depreciation

A   10.   Office Equipment

X   11.   Revenue

X   12.   Rent Expense

X   13.   Income Summary

A   14.   Prepaid Insurance

A   15.   Interest Payable

Self-Test 5: Identify the Financial Statement Accounts (Page 84)

1. __A__ Cash

2. __A__ Prepaid Rent

3. __L__ Accounts Payable

4. __E__ Supplies Used

5. __A__ Investments

6. __L__ Notes Payable

7. __A__ Supplies

8. __OE__ Capital

9. __A__ Equipment

10. __E__ Wage Expense

11. __OE__ Withdrawal

12. __E__ Utilities Expense

13. __A__ Buildings

14. __L__ Wage Payable

15. __A__ Land

Self-Test 6: Identify Statements (Page 85)

	Income Statement		Balance Sheet	
	Debit	Credit	Debit	Credit
1. Accounts Payable				X
2. Capital				X
3. Cash			X	
4. Salaries Payable				X
5. Prepaid Insurance			X	
6. Dental Fees		X		
7. Accounts Receivable			X	
8. Telephone Expense	X			
9. Withdrawals			X	
10. Land			X	
11. Salary Expense	X			
12. Office Supplies			X	
13. Notes Payable				X
14. Interest Payable				X

Self-Test 7: Classifying Balance Sheet Accounts (Page 86)

1. ___E___ Salaries Payable

2. ___G___ Capital

3. ___F___ Mortgage Payable

4. ___C___ Parking Lot

5. ___A___ Accounts Receivable

6. ___B___ Note Receivable (two years)

7. ___C___ Land

8. ___B___ Invested in Long-Term Bonds

9. ___G___ Withdrawals

10. ___I___ Wages Earned by Employees

11. ___E___ Note Payable (due in two weeks)

VERN